W9-CDB-464

A+ books

Alphabet Fun

Z Is for *Zoom!*

A Race Car Alphabet

by Laura Purdie Salas

Capstone *press*

A is for announcer.

"Ladies and gentlemen, start your engines!" An announcer starts the race. Who's in the lead? Who just crashed? The announcer keeps the crowd up to speed.

2

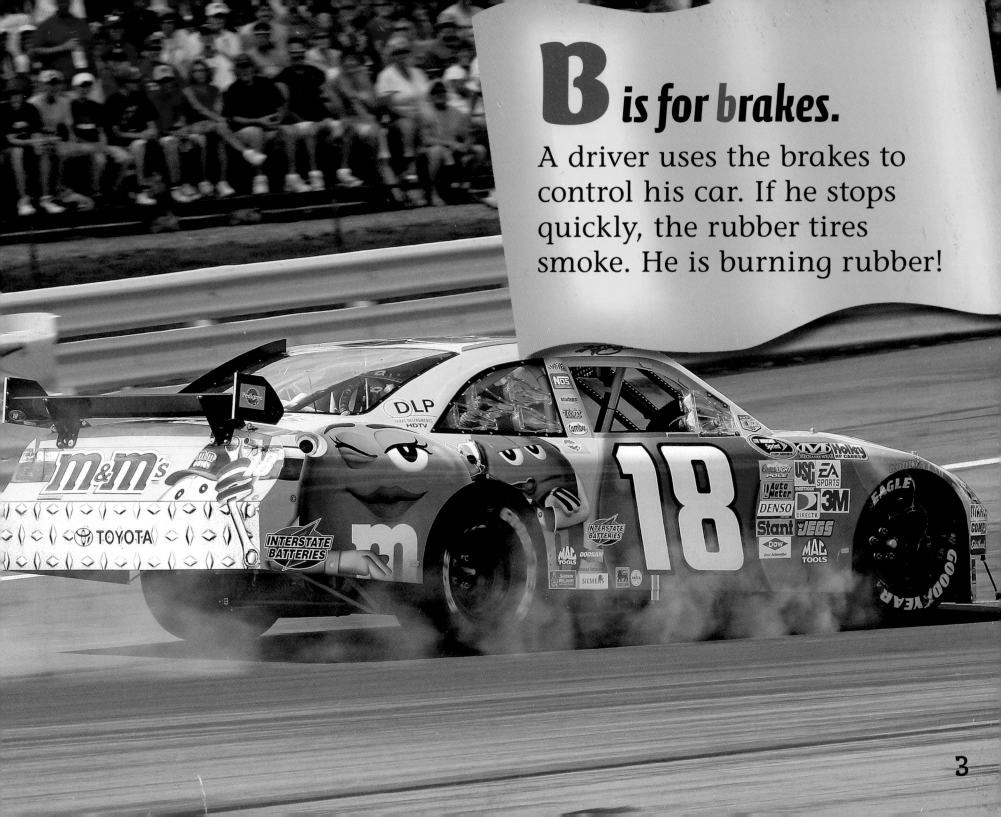

B is for brakes.

A driver uses the brakes to control his car. If he stops quickly, the rubber tires smoke. He is burning rubber!

3

C is for checkered flag.

The flagman waves a
checkered flag to show
a driver has won the race.
It's time for the winner
to celebrate!

4

D is for driver.

Race car drivers have to be in great shape. High speed is hard on their bodies. They must build strong neck, chest, and stomach muscles.

5

E *is for exhaust.*

The motor uses up most of the gasoline. The leftover gas goes out exhaust pipes. Exhaust is invisible, so you can only see it when it catches fire.

F *is for finish line.*

The first driver to cross the finish line wins. Sometimes drivers cross at almost the same moment. Photos show who crossed first and won.

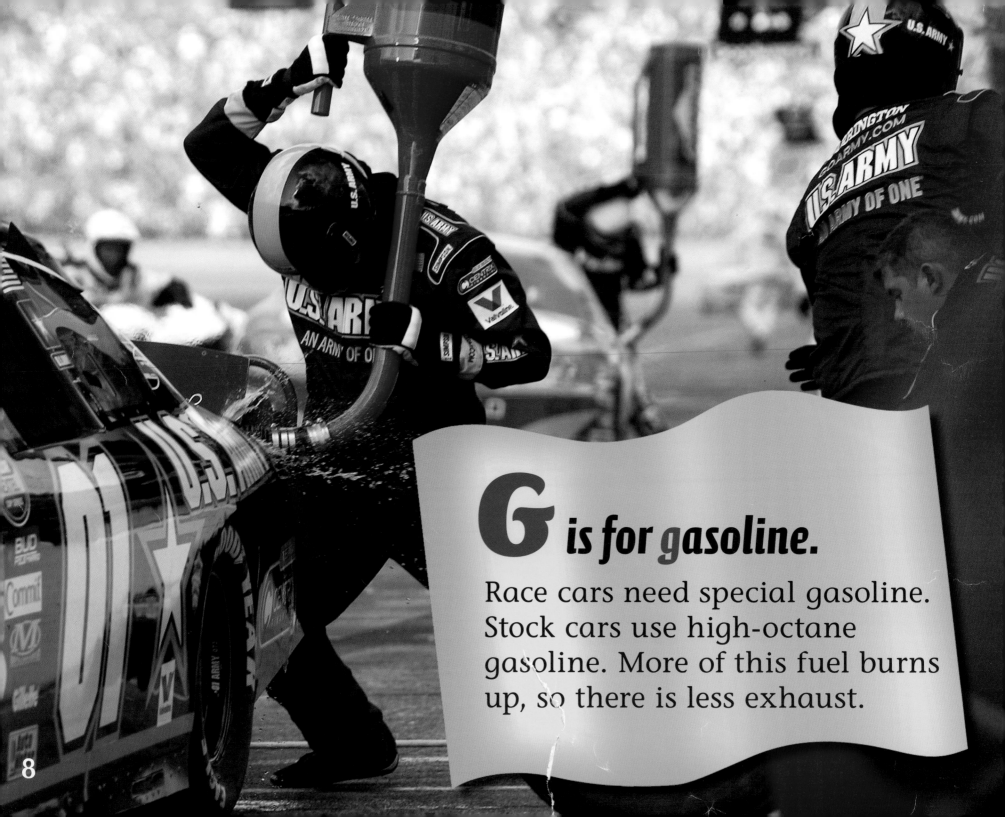

G is for gasoline.

Race cars need special gasoline. Stock cars use high-octane gasoline. More of this fuel burns up, so there is less exhaust.

H is for helmet

Race car drivers wear helmets to protect their heads. In a crash, a helmet can save a driver's life.

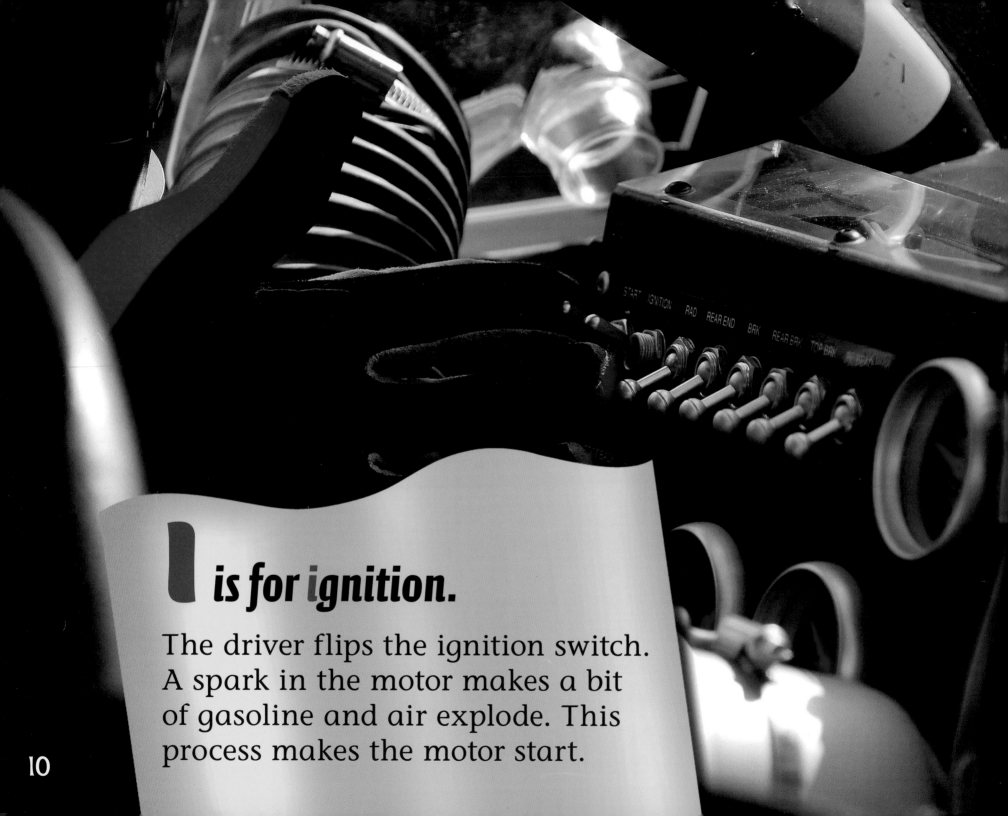

I is for ignition.

The driver flips the ignition switch. A spark in the motor makes a bit of gasoline and air explode. This process makes the motor start.

J is for jack.

The pit crew uses a jack. This lever raises the heavy car. Then the pit crew can change the tires.

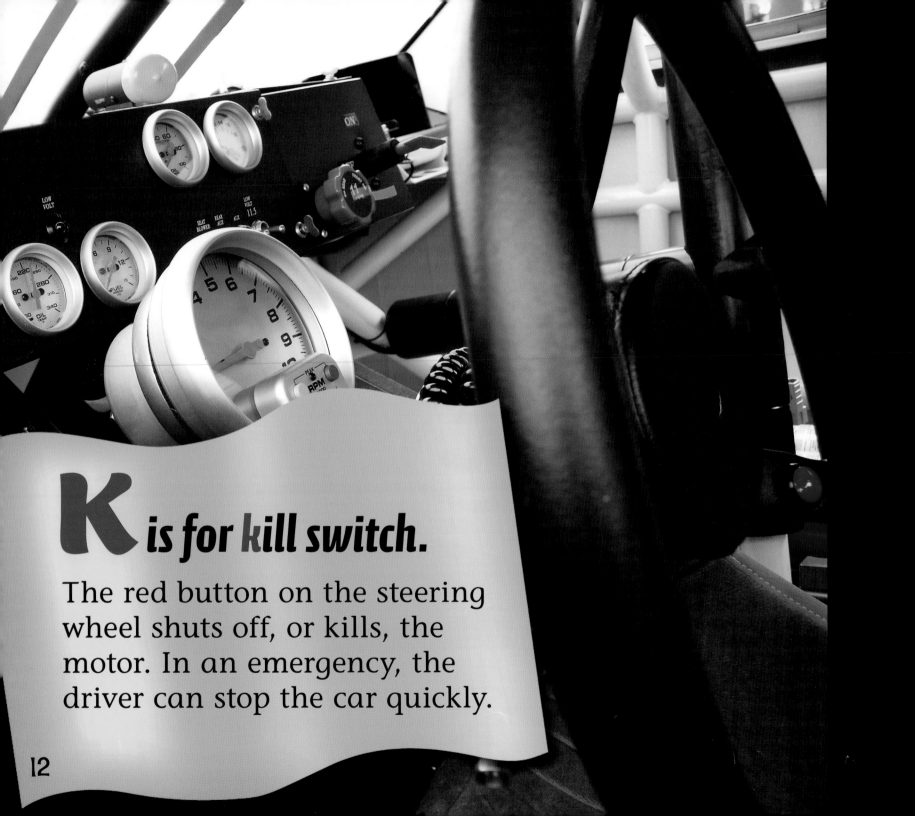

K *is for kill switch.*

The red button on the steering wheel shuts off, or kills, the motor. In an emergency, the driver can stop the car quickly.

L *is for* lights.

A stock car has a smooth, metal shell. It has no headlights. It just has stickers that look like headlights.

13

M *is for* **motor.**

The motor makes the race car go. Each piece fits perfectly. No air leaks out. No leaks make the car fast and powerful.

N is for net.

Race cars crash, flip, and roll. Window netting keeps the driver's head and arms inside the car.

O is for oval.

Many race tracks are oval. At the Daytona 500, drivers race 200 oval laps. That is 500 miles (805 kilometers).

P is for pit stop.

A driver makes a pit stop when the car needs work. A pit crew can change the tires and add gasoline in just 15 seconds!

17

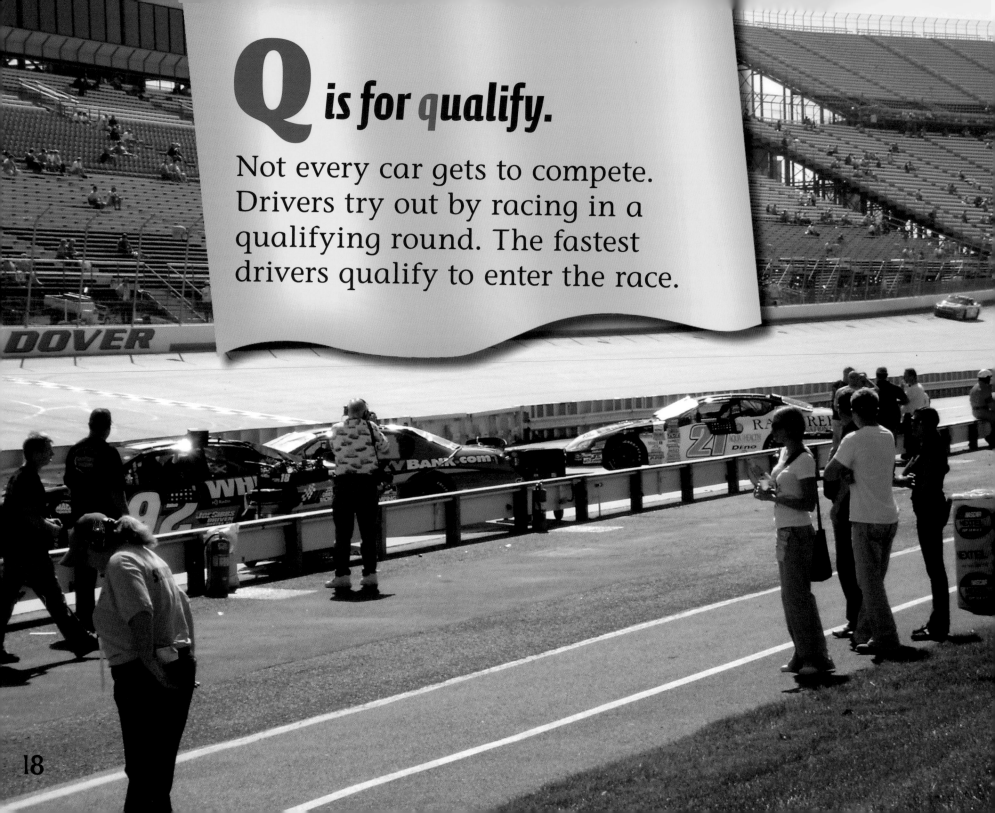

Q is for qualify.

Not every car gets to compete. Drivers try out by racing in a qualifying round. The fastest drivers qualify to enter the race.

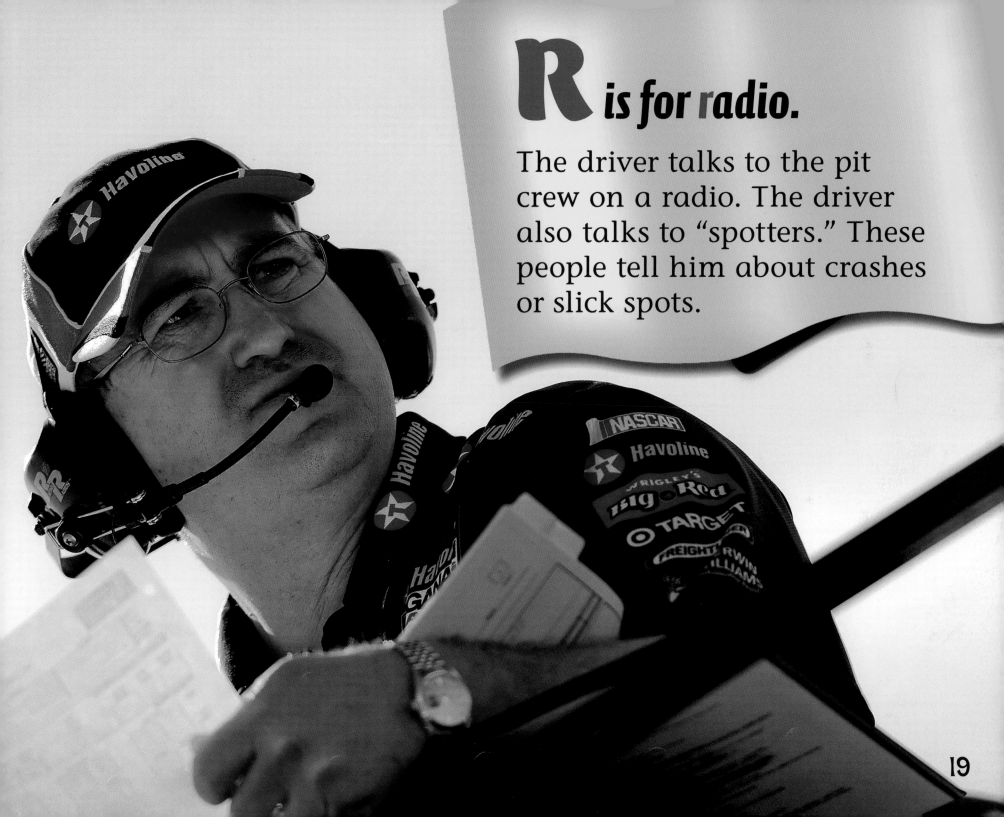

R *is for radio.*

The driver talks to the pit crew on a radio. The driver also talks to "spotters." These people tell him about crashes or slick spots.

19

S *is for* seat belt.

All drivers wear seat belts. Strong straps over both shoulders hold the driver in place.

T is for tires.

Smooth tires grip the track. Most tires have a second tire inside. If one tire blows, the driver can still drive to the pit stop.

U is for uniform.

Race car drivers and crews wear uniforms with their team name. A special uniform helps keep the driver safe. Its cloth doesn't catch fire easily.

V is for victory lap.

After a race ends, the winner takes a victory lap. He drives around the racetrack one more time while the crowd cheers.

23

W is for winner.

The first person across the finish line wins a trophy and money. The Daytona 500 winner gets more than $1.5 million!

X is for extreme speed.

Racing is all about speed. Race cars can go more than 220 miles (354 kilometers) per hour. That's four times faster than cars driving on the highway!

Y is for yellow flag.

A yellow caution flag means the track is dangerous. Maybe two cars crashed or the track is slippery. Drivers must stay behind a pace car.

Z *is for* zoom.

Motors revving! Flags flying! Pit crews dashing! Cars speeding! A racetrack is an exciting place to be. Zoom! Zoom!

Fun Facts about Race Cars

Lots of race car drivers start out racing in small vehicles called karts. They start as young as age 8.

Many race car drivers use computer exercises and video games to sharpen their skills. Practice on the computer can really pay off on the track.

Many drivers exercise in hot rooms. This training gets them ready for the high temperatures inside their race cars.

Some race cars have a spoiler on the back. A spoiler is a curved strip of metal. When the car reaches high speeds, the spoiler presses down on the car. It helps keep the car on the track.

Have you ever wondered how brakes work? When drivers press the brake pedal, it makes parts of the car rub against the wheels. That slows the wheels down, which slows the car.

Usually race cars use smooth tires with no tread cut into them. These are called "slicks." But when the track is wet, tires with treads are used. They are called "wets."

Drivers have sometimes hit the kill switch by accident. It's hard to tell whether the button is in the on or off position. The drivers thought their cars just stopped working.

Glossary

control (kuhn-TROHL) – to have power over something

emergency (i-MUR-juhn-see) – something that calls for a fast reaction

exhaust (eg-ZAWST) – the waste gases that come out of a car

explode (ek-SPLODE) – to blow apart with a loud bang and great force

invisible (in-VIZ-uh-buhl) – something you cannot see

pace car (PAYSS kar) – a car that other drivers may not pass when the yellow flag is raised

pit stop (PIT stop) – to drive a race car off the track so the pit crew can change tires, add gasoline, and do any other work

shell (SHEL) – the outer case of a car that covers the motor and other parts

spark (SPARK) – a tiny bit of flame

stock car (STOK CAR) – a car for racing, made from a regular car sold to the public

tread (TRED) – a ridge on a car's tire that helps the tire grip the road

Read More

Pipe, Jim. *Racing Cars.* Read and Play. Mankato, Minn.: Stargazer, 2009.

Schuette, Sarah L. *Hot Rods.* Horsepower. Mankato, Minn.: Capstone Press, 2007.

Zobel, Derek. *Race Cars.* Mighty Machines. Minneapolis: Bellweather Media, 2010.

Internet Sites

FactHound offers a safe, fun way to find Internet sites related to this book. All of the sites on FactHound have been researched by our staff.

Here's all you do:

Visit *www.facthound.com*

FactHound will fetch the best sites for you!

Index

Note to Parents, Teachers, and Librarians

Alphabet Fun books use bold art and photographs and topics with high appeal to engage young children in learning. Compelling nonfiction content educates and entertains while propelling readers toward mastery of the alphabet. These books are designed to be read aloud to a pre-reader or read independently by an early reader. The images help children understand the text and concepts discussed. Alphabet Fun books support further learning by including the following sections: Fun Facts, Glossary, Read More, Internet Sites, and Index. Early readers may need assistance using these features.

 Books published by Capstone Press are manufactured with paper containing at least 10 percent post-consumer waste.

A+ Books are published by Capstone Press, 151 Good Counsel Drive, P.O. Box 669, Mankato, Minnesota 56002.
www.capstonepress.com

Printed in the United States of America

Library of Congress Cataloging-in-Publication Data
Salas, Laura Purdie.
   Z is for zoom! : a race car alphabet / by Laura Purdie Salas.
   p. cm. — (A+. Alphabet fun)
   Includes bibliographical references and index.
   Summary: "Introduces car racing through photographs and brief text that uses one word relating to car racing for each letter of the alphabet" — Provided by publisher.
   ISBN-13 978-1-4296-3294-2 (library binding)
   ISBN-13 978-1-4296-3850-0 (paperback)
   1. Automobiles, Racing — Juvenile literature. 2. Alphabet books — Juvenile literature. I. Title. II. Series.
TL236.S285 2010
796.72 — dc22   2009010197

Credits
Jenny Marks, editor; Tracy Davies, designer; Marcie Spence, media researcher

Photo Credits
Getty Images Inc./Al Bello, 6
iStockphoto/Eric Hood, cover, 7; Hirkophoto, 21; jacomstephens, 13; Michael Krinke, 12; Michael_at_isp, 4; nycshooter, 14
Newscom, 1, 5, 8, 10, 11, 20, 22, 26; Bob Leverone/TSN/Icon SMI, 2; Cal Sport Media, 25; Jared C. Tilton/ASP Inc., 9; photographer, 19; Tom Whitmore/Icon SMI, 3; Walter G. Arce/Cal Sport Media ABACAUSA, 16
Shutterstock/Alexey Stiop, 27; bsankow, 18; Christopher Halloran, 15; Tiago Hora, 24; Todd Taulman, 17, 23